LEAVING A LEGACY
INSTEAD OF A MESS

ESTATE PLANNING WITH LIVING TRUSTS

SUREN G. ADAMS

Copyright © Suren G. Adams

All rights reserved. No part of this publication may be reproduced, distributed, or transmitted in any form or by any means, including photocopying, recording, or other electronic methods, without the prior written consent of the publisher and author, with the exception of brief quotations used for reviews and certain noncommercial uses allowed by copyright law. For all permission requests, write to the publisher at the address below.

ISBN-13: 978-1540782090

Jackson
PUBLISHING
LET THE WORDS CHANGE YOU

Table of Contents

Chapter One Estate Planning 101 1

Chapter Two The Probate Process – Why it Should be Avoided 7

Chapter Three Identifying Your Estate and The Ideal Planning Candidate 13

Chapter Four A Faulty Plan Versus a GOOD Estate Plan 19

Chapter Five The Benefits of Living Trusts 30

Chapter Six Terms You Should Know 41

Chapter Seven The Simple Summary 45

Chapter One

Estate Planning 101

Why Focus on Estate Planning?

Many people believe that they do not have "enough" to need an "Estate Plan." Whether you were born into massive wealth, built your own fortune, or have nothing more than a cat or the clothes on your back, you still need an Estate Plan if you are over 18 years old. Why? Because an Estate Plan is not just about planning what happens to your money after you're gone; a GOOD Estate Plan creates the roadmap your loved ones can follow for:

- Who you want to handle your medical and financial decisions if you can't;
- What you want that person to do and when;
- Who should take care of your children if you can't and how they should be cared for;
- How assets like life insurance should be distributed to your loved ones and when;
- And so much more.

Many of the details in an Estate Plan deal with your wishes on things **other** than money, so it doesn't matter whether you have multi-millions or only $10.00 to your name. The primary goal of an Estate Plan is to make decisions about things concerning the management of your life, health and wealth while you are still able to make those decisions. You then write out those decisions in a legally binding way so that what you **want** to happen, actually **does** happen, rather than what the state legislature, court, or the loudest and bossiest family member decides *should* happen.

We all spend a lot of effort ensuring that we protect the things we acquire. We buy insurance policies, warranties, locks and security systems. We spend time and money on maintenance and upkeep. We have homeowners' associations and neighborhood watches. When it comes to our own health, well-being and independence, we do even more, including health club memberships, annual check-ups at the dentist, eye doctor, and primary care physicians. We buy organic foods and try countless weight loss plans, vitamins or supplements. The list goes on and on. When it comes to our children, the list of extras is endless: sports camps, teams, leagues, dance lessons, swim lessons, instruments, karate, tutors, SAT prep, health insurance, car insurance, helmets and protective gear in every form. Yet, we assume that nothing will ever happen to us! We protect everything and everyone, knowing that bad things can happen, but we still act as if we will always be here, healthy and ready to do what we've always been doing. We cannot assume that things will magically happen just the way they should or just the way we want them to if we cannot be there in person and in our right minds to make sure of it. As with all the other areas of our lives, we need to put things in order to make sure that our loved ones and our things will be protected and, more importantly, that our plans, dreams and wishes are respected!

What Will Happen to My Estate if I Don't Plan Properly?

If you do not create an Estate Plan for yourself, then the state will create one for you. Your first reaction may be to think that the state-created plan "couldn't be *that* bad." However, you would be wrong. Here is just **one** example of what the Maryland state legislature has come up with if you pass away without an Estate Plan and you are married, without any children, and your parents or parent are alive. Your spouse gets $15,000.00 plus 50% of your remaining estate and **your parents** get the other 50%! Hopefully, your spouse gets along with their in-laws now, because they probably won't be so friendly after that kind of distribution. The laws that designate who gets what if you pass away without an Estate Plan are called intestacy laws. You don't want these laws to be applied to the assets you worked hard to get or to the family you worked so hard to protect.

Even if it doesn't matter to you what happens to your spouse after you're gone, I know that you care about what happens to your children. If both parents pass away without an Estate Plan, the court then decides who takes care of your children. Generally, this means that the loudest, bossiest family member takes control of the situation and usually gets their way by presenting the "most compelling" case. This is probably **not** how you want the guardian of your children to be selected.

What about if you are injured or ill, but do not pass away? If you don't have an Estate Plan, you are essentially asking your loved ones to commit forgery, mail fraud, and bank fraud just to get your mail open and your bills paid! You have to put a legally binding Durable Power of Attorney in place while you are competent in order to appoint someone to manage your affairs if you are incapacitated (unable to act for yourself due to your mental or physical condition or whereabouts). If you wait until something happens, then it is too late to get a Durable Power of

Attorney. Your loved ones have to go through a costly guardianship case to have the court name someone to legally act on your behalf (another opportunity for that loud and bossy family member to gain control of your affairs). One of the saddest client consultations I have had in my career was with a woman in her mid-forties who recently became the primary caregiver for her aging mother (who was only in her late sixties). The mother had been diagnosed with dementia and her competence quickly deteriorated. By the time they got to my office for an Estate Plan so that the daughter could handle her mother's finances, the older woman could not answer basic questions about where we were, who her family members were, and what assets she owned. Question after question was answered incorrectly, even though my questions were getting more and more basic. At that point, it was too late to create an Estate Plan – the mother was no longer competent to do so. A guardianship case was the only remaining **legal** option, which would prove embarrassing to the mother, costly for the daughter (certainly more than a detailed Estate Plan would be), and time-consuming for everyone involved.

Without a good Estate Plan, your estate will also have to go through probate. We will take some time to describe probate in the next chapter so that you know why it's important to avoid it, if at all possible.

Chapter Two

The Probate Process – Why it Should be Avoided

What is Probate?

Probate is the court-supervised process of distributing your assets to other people after you pass away. If you have NO Estate Plan or if you just have a Will Estate Plan, your estate will have to go through probate. Most people assume that if they get a Will, they can avoid probate, but that's not the case. If you have a Will, but do not also have a Trust or one of the other methods below that address all of your assets, your estate will still go through probate. The best way to understand this is to think about your car. If, for example, you have a car that is in your name and you pass away, there has to be a legal way to transfer the title for that vehicle to someone else. Even if your Will says, "Give my car to my spouse after I die," someone has to sign the title over to your spouse. The person who does this is the Executor or Personal Representative named in your Will or appointed by the court, if you don't have a Will. The issue is that even if your Will names that

Executor, the court has to approve their appointment and give them legal authority (Letter of Administration with the court seal) to act on behalf of your estate; otherwise, anyone could transfer your assets before you even pass away simply by showing what you said in your Will.

If you pass away without a Will, your estate goes through intestacy probate, as we mentioned before. That is when the intestacy rules apply to the distribution of your assets in probate.

Why Avoid Probate?

The primary reasons to avoid probate are: 1) it is time consuming and delays distributions; 2) it is costly; and 3) it is public. Although the probate process has been streamlined from the "olden days," it is still no picnic. In Maryland, the minimum timeframe for a regular estate is 7 months, but most estates take about a year or more to fully probate. This can cause a delay in distributing assets to beneficiaries, as the Executor will want to make sure that all valid claims against the estate are paid prior to distributions.

The probate process can also be quite costly. For example, in a $500,000.00 Maryland estate, the Personal Representative's commissions/attorney's fees alone can be over $20,000.00! With average property values in Maryland, estates can quickly be in that range with just the value of real estate, which can often force beneficiaries to sell family homes just to cover the basic costs of a probate estate. When compared with the average cost of a good estate plan, which is between $2,000.00 and $5,000.00, paying 5 to 10 times that much in probate costs doesn't make much sense.

An issue that is often overlooked is the public nature of probate. The fact that predatory individuals can access an estate file and see who the beneficiaries of an estate are, including when they will be receiving assets, and how much, is problematic to say the least.

Ways to Avoid Probate

The best part about probate is that it can be avoided! There are several ways to avoid probate, although there are potential issues with all but one of the ways:

- **Joint Tenancy**

Joint tenancy is pretty familiar to most people because it's usually how you own your home if you are married. If you own something as a joint tenant, and the other owner passes away, you inherit the property entirely. That property passes to the surviving owner WITHOUT going through probate. The issue comes up when the surviving owner passes away. Just like the car example above, there is no way to transfer the deed for that property after the surviving owner dies, without getting the court-approved legal authority to do so. Even if a couple both say in their Wills: "After we die, give our house to our children," in order for the children to get the house, it has to go through probate after the last spouse passes away. If you throw in the common wrinkle of a second marriage and no Estate Plan, we then have a situation where the original children of a marriage can end up being disinherited. Here is an example of how that can happen…

Joe and Jane marry and have 2 children. They buy a house and live happily with their children until Jane passes away unexpectedly. The children grow up and move away to go to college. Their dad eventually gets remarried to Mary. After years of Mary paying half of the mortgage and helping with maintenance and upkeep, Joe adds Mary to the deed as a joint tenant. He also prepares an online Will saying that he wants the house to go to his children if he passes away. Thinking that he has covered all his bases, he happily carries on, until many years later, when he passes away. Mary will then inherit the house entirely. The house will pass outside of probate because she is a joint tenant. Mary then passes away a few years later, and most people would assume, surely the house now goes to Joe and Jane's children, right? Wrong. If Mary never created a Will, then the house will pass according to the intestacy rules to Mary's children she had prior to marrying Joe, after going through probate. This is a sad result that happens all the time due to poor planning or no planning. The saddest part is that the result is completely avoidable.

- **Beneficiary Designation**

Most people are familiar with this type of estate-planning technique because employers and insurance companies will usually require you to name a beneficiary on certain types of accounts or policies, such as 401Ks, IRAs or life insurance. When you designate a beneficiary on an account or policy, upon your passing, that asset gets distributed to the beneficiary without going through probate. There are several problems with people depending solely on this technique for estate planning. A primary issue is that if you have minor beneficiaries (children under the age of 18), they can gain full control over the assets they inherit through beneficiary designations when they turn 18. When I think back to when I was 18, it would have been the worst time for me to inherit any kind of lump sum of money. Usually, this means that the 18-year-old will blow all of the money on a fast car, shopping, and parties with their friends. Not school, not books, not buying a house, and not saving for their wedding or for emergencies – not a chance!

Another potential pitfall with beneficiary designations is keeping them updated. Over the years, I have met with so many couples where the husband (sorry guys, 90% of the time it's the husband) still has his parent/parents listed as the beneficiary on his life insurance at work. Another issue is if the named beneficiary does not survive the owner of the policy. That life insurance then has to go through probate to get distributed to whomever is named in the Will or through the intestacy rules, if there is no Will.

- **Revocable or Irrevocable Trust**

    By far the best method for avoiding probate, intestacy rules, and the other issues that we've talked about is a Trust Estate Plan. We will go over the details of this type of plan a bit later. Now, we will go over how to create your Estate Plan.

Chapter Three

Identifying Your Estate and

The Ideal Planning Candidate

What Items Compose an Estate?

Your "estate" is basically made up of all your "stuff" and everything over which you have control.

Here is a simple list of what makes up an estate – some of which may surprise you:

- Household property, such as furniture, decorative items, artwork, and china
- Jewelry, furs, and clothing of value
- Vehicles, such as cars, motorcycles, boats, RVs and trailers
- Real estate, including your primary residence, vacation homes and timeshares
- Financial accounts, including checking and savings bank accounts, as well as investment accounts, such as mutual funds, stocks, bonds and certificates of deposits

- Retirement accounts, such as IRAs, 401(k)s and annuities
- AND life insurance

Yes, life insurance is included in an estate. It is important to know that because state and federal governments include life insurance in their calculation of your estate for estate tax purposes. In order to know if you will be subject to estate taxes, you need to know the size of your estate. You calculate the size of your estate by adding up the value of the items listed previously that make up your estate.

As of 2016, if the size of your estate is more than $5.45 million, the federal estate tax that applies to the portion of your estate over that $5.45 million is 40%! For example, if your estate size is $10 million, your federal estate tax liability would be $1.82 million ($10 million - $5.45 million x 40%). That's a significant tax bill and a large chunk of your estate going to Uncle Sam, rather than your children. Of course, there are various estate-planning techniques that you can use to postpone, minimize or completely eliminate estate taxes. We will briefly touch on some of these techniques later.

In Maryland, as of 2016, the state estate tax is approximately 16% for estates over $2 million. In 2016, in the District of Columbia, estate tax kicks in for estates over $1 million! Given the property values in the

Washington metropolitan area, it's very easy for estates to hit these local thresholds. Add in life insurance from your employer and any separate life insurance policies that you may have, and you can quickly see how important it is to know the size of your estate so that you can prepare a proper Estate Plan.

If your estate is well under the threshold for applying estate taxes, it is even more important to protect what you have. Essentially, the less you have, the more you should be trying to protect it. Proper planning is even more important to you and your family because you're going to need everything you can! Estate taxes may not apply, but probate costs and delays can quickly eat up an estate even faster. We will discuss probate avoidance soon, but when it comes to either estate taxes or probate costs and delay, the best solution is a good Estate Plan.

So, Who Needs an Estate Plan Then?

As you've probably guessed by now, every adult (anyone over the age of 18) needs an Estate Plan, regardless of your marital status, how much older than 18 you are, whether you have children, or the size of your estate.

Single People

As a single, unmarried person, you especially need to decide **who** will manage your estate if you become incapacitated or pass away. There is no "standard" person, like a spouse, that the court would identify as the guardian of your person and property. Once again, cue the loud and bossy family member. When I was single, I was fiercely independent. I remember strapping an Ikea sofa into the trunk of my Volkswagen Paseo and pulling it up to my third-floor apartment BY MYSELF when I was single. I was very proud of that madness, so if you had told me back then that anyone besides me would be making decisions about my health care, my finances or anything else in my life, I would have gone nuts. Single people should protect their independence and their wishes because that is really the biggest benefit of being single. If you have a favorite charity, family member or other beneficiary, or any kind of plan that doesn't line up with the state intestacy laws, then you must have a legally binding Estate Plan or that plan will NOT happen.

Married People Without Children

Most married couples assume that if one of them passes away, their spouse will receive everything. Without an Estate Plan, however, that may not be the case. If you have any separately owned assets, such as vehicles or bank accounts, those assets will be distributed according to the state's intestacy laws. As described previously, the Maryland intestacy laws state that if you are married, without children, and your parent/parents are still alive, your spouse will receive roughly 50% of your estate. Your spouse fairs better in DC, where they will receive 75% of the estate, while parents receive 25%. Only a legally binding Estate Plan will cause the estate to be distributed 100% to your spouse in these jurisdictions, if your parents are also alive.

Married People With Children

Most married couples with children also assume that if something happens to one of them, their spouse will inherit everything, ensuring that they can take care of the children and do things like pay off mortgages, etc. In Maryland, if this happens without an Estate Plan in place, and you have minor children, your spouse will get 50% of the estate and your children will get the other 50%! This means that a custodial account will need to be set up for their share, and when they turn 18, they will have complete control over that money. As mentioned before, that is the worst possible time to inherit a lump sum of money.

In Maryland, if your children are over 18 when you pass away, your spouse will get $15,000 and 50% of the remaining estate, while your children get the other 50%. They get that 50% share in their hands immediately after the estate goes through probate. Once again, this is probably NOT a wise choice for an 18-year-old.

Chapter Four

A Faulty Plan Versus a GOOD Estate Plan

What Makes a GOOD Estate Plan?

Once you have made the important decision to establish an Estate Plan, be sure that you do not set up a bad Estate Plan. The difference between the two can mean tens of thousands of dollars to your beneficiaries. It is the difference between things actually happening the way you intend or not. A good plan means that you can leave a legacy and ensure family peace, rather than leaving a MESS! Basically, this is not the time to bargain shop. You are protecting the things that are most important to you – your family and everything else that you have worked to acquire. Once you find out if a bargain basement Estate Plan actually works, it will be too late and your family will be left cleaning up the mess that you wasted your money and time on.

There are several ways to ensure that you have a good estate plan:

1) Pick a reputable and experienced ESTATE PLANNING attorney to prepare your Estate Plan. When reviewing attorneys, look for feedback from their former clients. You should be able

to get this upon request from the firm, online via various attorney directories, or on the firm's website. Also, be sure that the attorney actually has experience preparing the type of Estate Plan that you need. Every lawyer takes an estate-planning course in law school and can access practice manuals from their local Bar Associations, so if you ask most lawyers if they "do Wills," they will say, "Yes, of course." However, you do not want a boilerplate document for your Estate Plan. If that were the case, you might as well get an online do-it-yourself Will. What you want is a state-of-the-art plan incorporating current laws and cases. There is WAY too much that is constantly changing in this area of law to depend on a basic online or boilerplate document to protect your family and assets.

2) Be detailed about your family situation, assets and concerns when meeting with your attorney. This is where your plan becomes tailor-made for your specific situation. If you leave out that piece of land in South Carolina that you inherited from Grandma, then there will be a gaping hole in your plan that will cause major issues for your family down the road.

3) Review and update your plan frequently. If you can sign up for some type of a maintenance plan with your attorney, do it. If that isn't available, do your own annual review of your plan and look for things like:

- Are there new family members that need to be added or other beneficiaries that need to be added or removed due to death or a change in circumstances or relationships?

- Are the agents you selected for various roles still the people that you want to serve in those roles? Is their contact information still correct?

- Are there new titled assets (assets that have a deed, title or other evidence of ownership), policies or accounts that need to added to your Estate Plan? Have the previously owned assets all been retitled or addressed in your Estate Plan?

- Are there any changes in the law that require a change in your plan (this is where an annual maintenance plan initiated by your attorney becomes really beneficial)?

A GOOD Estate Plan should carefully detail the following in a legally binding way:

- ✓ Who should look after your estate upon your death or incapacity
- ✓ Who gets what and how it all should be divided
- ✓ How the assets should be distributed
- ✓ Who should care for minor or incapacitated dependents and how they should receive the assets you leave them
- ✓ Provide a plan for how to preserve your assets for the next generation or your designated beneficiaries, which may include charitable organizations

Reasons to Put Together an Estate Plan

- ✓ To avoid probate
- ✓ To reduce or delay estate taxes
- ✓ To effectively manage your assets and your health decisions in the case of incapacity
- ✓ To prevent family strife and confusion
- ✓ To avoid intestacy laws
- ✓ To protect your children and loved ones

The more sophisticated your Estate Plan, the more control you will have over your assets while you are alive and following your death. In essence, you want to protect your assets and ensure that your beneficiaries receive exactly what you want them to and how.

Estate planning is not just good stewardship of your finances; it is good stewardship of your relationships.

How Do You Put Together an Estate Plan?

The best plans start with a good deal of thought before ever walking into a lawyer's office. Think about who you want to benefit when you pass away and what you would want them to do with what you leave them. Then, think about who you can trust to carry out your wishes. That is usually the same person or people that are designated to act on your behalf while you are alive, but incapacitated. If you have children, think about who you would want to care for them if you were unable. Also, think about the general value of your assets and get a rough total in mind, INCLUDING LIFE INSURANCE. Those big questions are the "meat" of your plan, meaning that everything will build off of those answers. If you cannot nail down answers to all of these questions, at least think about them, so that when meeting with your attorney, they can help walk you through the issues and jointly come up with the best options for you and your family. They will also have pointers that will help with the decisions, so don't let unanswered questions stop you from proceeding or setting a meeting. The process of thinking about these issues is the first step, not the last.

Allow enough time for your meeting with the attorney. In my firm, we periodically offer estate-planning seminars where we discuss all the important things to know about estate planning. Clients who are able to attend a seminar before their consultation find that we can "dive right in" during their consultations and cover a lot of the specifics related to their plan during our initial meeting. If you're reading this book, you will be able to do the same thing when you go into a consultation regarding your estate plan.

If you have done your research to find a good estate-planning attorney, you should be able to leave the rest of the work to your lawyer. After providing all the details you can in the consultation and any documentation requested by your attorney, your role is to thoroughly review the prepared plan to be sure it represents what you discussed. A good attorney will take the facts and prepare the legal documents that you need before explaining them to you in layman's terms.

If you are still tempted to buy a do-it-yourself plan, you do so at your own risk. You don't know what you don't know. You might do everything you're told to do in a software program or online, yet you still might have a huge gaping hole in your plan, simply because you didn't know that you needed to address a certain situation in your jurisdiction or for your family's particular situation.

What Documents are needed for an Estate Plan?

Every Estate Plan needs to have certain documents in order to address incapacity and end-of-life wishes, along with all the other things we've discussed. <u>These are the documents that should be included in your Estate Plan:</u>

A Durable Power of Attorney

This is the legal document that names the person who should handle your financial affairs if you are unable to do so yourself. This document is "durable" because it can be used even if you are incapacitated mentally or physically; however, it cannot be used after your death. The Durable Power of Attorney can be used for things like writing checks from your accounts, collecting and opening your mail, closing or opening accounts, completing tax returns, and even caring for pets.

The Advanced Healthcare Directive and Living Will

The Advanced Healthcare Directive names the person who should handle your medical decisions if you are unable to do so yourself. The

Living Will states what your wishes are for end of life, so if you are incapacitated and unable to state what you want to happen, the Living Will can provide guidance to your Advanced Directive Agent. In this document, you can specify whether you want to die naturally, without any artificial medical treatment, or if you want to use all available artificial medical treatment, or perhaps just food and water artificially. With the Directive and Living Will, you should also have a HIPAA (Health Insurance Portability and Accountability Act) Authorization, which allows you to name the person/persons who should have access to your medical records to assist in making medical decisions or advocating for your interests if you are unable to do so. If you want to be an organ donor, an Organ Donor Addendum should also be included in your Estate Plan to specify your wishes for organ donation.

The Last Will and Testament

Despite the fact that a Will does not necessarily prevent probate, you still need to have one in your Estate Plan. If you have a Trust Plan, the Will becomes a catchall document and is referred to as a Pour-Over Will, because it pours any assets that aren't retitled to the Trust into the Trust after your passing. That has to happen through probate, so it's supposed to serve as a back-up document in this type of plan. The Will is also where you name the guardian for your minor children and where you specify your wishes regarding burial versus cremation.

If you don't have a Trust, your Will should also name who gets what in your estate after it goes through probate. Your will also names who you want to be the Executor or Personal Representative of your estate.

A Will can also have a Testamentary Trust in it. A Testamentary Trust is the type of Trust that comes into existence after your passing. The estate first goes through probate, and then into the Trust to be distributed to your beneficiaries.

It is important to remember that if you have assets in your Will that are intended to be distributed to beneficiaries, those assets will be going through probate first.

A Revocable or Irrevocable Trust

We will talk about revocable living trusts in detail in the next chapter. An irrevocable Trust is the type of Trust that cannot be changed once it is created. Because it cannot be changed, it is only used for assets that you will not eventually need. Irrevocable trusts are generally used in larger estates for the purpose of taking assets out of the control of a person who needs to reduce their federal estate tax exposure. As of

2016, that is usually for estates over $11 million. A specific type of irrevocable Trust that can be used to reduce or eliminate state estate tax exposure is the Irrevocable Life Insurance Trust (ILIT). With an ILIT, you can remove a life insurance policy from your estate size, while still designating the beneficiaries and how the policy should be distributed to those beneficiaries.

I have a client who took advantage of this type of Trust to make sure her entire estate will be distributed to her children. She has a primary residence valued at about $750,000 and owns the home her mother lives in worth $500,000. She also has other liquid assets, such as bank accounts and investments, as well as two insurance policies, one for $1 million and another for $2 million, for her children. That $2 million policy would put her estate over the Maryland estate tax exemption, so it would be taxed at about 16%. That tax would mean that $320,000 less would be paid out to her children upon her death. So, we put that policy into an ILIT to prevent it from being included in her estate. Now, the entire estate can be distributed in full to her children.

The Revocable Living Trust is much more common because the Grantor maintains control of the assets in the Trust and the Trust is revocable – it can be changed at any time, provided that the Grantor is alive and competent. An important point to note is that a revocable living Trust is not an asset protection tool for the Grantor, because the Grantor still has control over the assets. If the Grantor can get to the assets, such as a bank account, it is the Grantor's asset and remains accessible by creditors of the Grantor. Umbrella insurance policies are good tools for protecting the assets of a Trust if you are concerned about potential litigation.

Chapter Five

The Benefits of Living Trusts

We have mentioned trusts throughout this book as the recommended type of Estate Plan, so let's explore these tools in more detail.

First, you need a good understanding of how a Trust works. A Trust is a legal agreement that creates a separate entity, similar to creating an LLC or a Corporation. Instead of this separate entity being used to own or manage a business, it will own and manage your personal assets (and can also own your business interests as well). You, as Grantor, transfer your assets into the name of the Trust that you control as Trustee while you are alive and competent. You are the beneficiary of your Trust while you are alive, so you can sell your assets, refinance, give away, and do whatever you currently do with your assets. You also name a successor Trustee or Trustees who will step into your shoes to manage the assets if you become incapacitated and who will distribute the assets after your passing to your beneficiaries in the way that you designate in the Trust Agreement.

Because the Trust owns all of your assets, when you pass away, there are no assets in your name to go through probate. That is how the Trust avoids probate. The Trust also contains thorough instructions addressing your specific family circumstances and distribution wishes, so it avoids intestacy rules. It also avoids the delay of probate and is a private document that does not have to be made part of the public record at the Register of Wills.

The List of Trust Benefits

Living Trusts are such great planning tools because of their many benefits:

- They avoid probate.
- They avoid guardianship proceedings by naming successor trustees who can manage your assets if you become incapacitated.
- They prevent distributions to minors or irresponsible beneficiaries.
- They allow distributions in a way that you determine, for the purposes you determine, and to whom you determine.
- They can serve as asset protection tools for beneficiaries if they are going through a divorce, tax issue, bankruptcy, or creditor issue at the time of receiving their bequest.

- They protect assets in second marriage scenarios from going to unintended beneficiaries.
- They protect assets in blended families so that they go where intended.
- They avoid state intestacy laws.
- They are private and avoid predatory schemes that are rampant in the probate process.
- They significantly reduce the possibility of someone winning if they contest your Estate Plan because the Trust is a living, functioning entity while you are alive and competent.
- They can protect assets for special needs beneficiaries to protect public benefits.
- They can prevent probate in multiple jurisdictions if you own assets in multiple jurisdictions.
- They have hundreds of years of legal history, dating back to the English feudal system, so they have established precedence and dependable treatment in the law.

Who are the People in a Trust?

The people involved in a Trust are the Grantor, Trustee, Successor Trustee, and Beneficiary. Let's go over each of these roles in detail.

The Grantor is sometimes also called the Settlor or the Trustor. This is the person who creates the Trust and puts their property into the name of the trust. This would be you.

Next you have the Trustee. The Trustee is the person who manages the Trust assets. This would also be you (while you are alive and competent to do so). If you are married, you will probably be creating a joint trust, in which case you will probably be serving as Co-Trustee with your spouse in your trust, with equal power and authority to manage the Trust assets. Generally, if there are Co-Trustees serving, either may act independently, but you can set up a Trust to state that Co-Trustees must agree on everything or to have more than 2 Co-Trustees.

The next role is the Successor Trustee. The Successor Trustee is the person that you name to step into your shoes when you have passed away or if you are incapacitated and cannot serve as Trustee. You should choose this person carefully. In a Trust Plan, the Trust is the primary planning tool of the plan and the Trustee and Successor Trustee are the agents who perform the key roles of the plan. A good Estate Plan will have multiple (at least 2) Successor Trustees and each should be someone whom you can trust (pardon the pun). Ideally, your successors will be good with finances, but if not, at least they should be wise enough to know when to hire a professional.

The final role is the beneficiary. The beneficiary is the person who receives the benefit of the Trust assets. That is also you, during your life. In your Trust, you also name beneficiaries of your Trust property after you pass away. You can name family members, friends, charitable organizations, schools, or whomever you would like. That is the beauty of an Estate Plan – you decide who should benefit from your years of hard work.

The beauty of a Trust Estate Plan is that you can decide HOW they get to benefit. This is the fun part! In a Trust Plan, you can be highly creative and customize your plan to your specific family situation. If you have one child who has chosen to be the proverbial starving artist, and will have no retirement savings at the end of their career, you can state that their Trust share will be distributed after they retire. You can determine what that retirement age will be. I had a client who created the most ingenious plan for a family member who had a substance abuse problem. Her Trust stated that the beneficiary would receive $200 per month if they passed a weekly drug test. If they passed 2 consecutive months of drug tests, the monthly amounts increased to $500. If they passed 6 consecutive months of drug tests, the monthly amounts increased to $1000. If they passed 12 consecutive months of drug tests, the monthly amounts increased to $3000. If at any time the beneficiary failed a drug test, the monthly amount dropped back down to $200 and the pattern would start all over again. It was a perfect way to steer behavior without forcing anyone to do anything. It provided positive motivation to act in a positive way, but did not provide so much that the beneficiary relied solely on the Trust for everything and stopped making an effort on their own. Brilliant!

As you would expect, most of the popular planning methods revolve around protecting assets for our children. There are two main approaches for how to distribute assets when you have more than 1 child. One is considered "fair" or "equal", while the other is considered to be more like "real life." One is not better than the other – it is strictly a preference. The option that is viewed as fair or equal consists of dividing the Trust assets equally among the children when the last parent dies. The other option mimics real life, because not everyone gets an equal share. After the last parent dies, the assets are kept in what is called a "common trust" and used for the care of all the children until the youngest child turns 18 or whatever age you determine. At that point, the Trust assets are divided among the children. That way, the bulk of the Trust property is made available for the most dependent of the children. If you do not have minor children, this is one less decision you would need to make.

Most parents distribute assets in a Trust to their children equally in the following way: whatever they need for their healthcare, education, maintenance, and support, and then 1/3 at 25, 30, and 35 years of age. With this approach, you can make sure that they do not inherit all of the assets at age 18 (like they would if you had no estate plan or just a Will) and irresponsibly blow it all. It also preserves the assets for the major life events that you would most likely want them to be using it for, such as getting started after college, getting married, buying their first home, or having children. Also, if they do end up spending their first lump sum unwisely, they will have 2 more opportunities to get it right.

Another great planning method is to require that your beneficiaries take a financial management course before receiving a lump sum bequest, or that they meet with your financial advisor first. This will help them be better educated and have the necessary tools to make wise decisions with the funds placed in their hands.

You can also require that your Trustee only distribute your Trust property for specific purposes, such as education, purchasing real estate or business development, so that you can guide behaviors in the direction you would like them to develop even after you are gone. Talk about leaving a legacy!

If you have a favorite charity, like St. Jude (a personal favorite) or your church congregation that you would like to benefit, you can also dictate this in your trust. You can either leave a lump sum for them to use for their normal charitable purposes or you can create a Charitable Trust with elaborate details about how the Trust property should be used for generations to come. These types of trusts can also remove assets from your estate size for estate tax purposes.

You can be as creative as your imagination allows when it comes to Trust planning, but the key is to have a good attorney who knows how to make your idea legally binding. Otherwise, what's the point? When you consult with your estate-planning lawyer, bring all of your ideas, hopes, dreams and concerns with you. Write them down so that you do not forget anything. Your attorney's job is to take those ideas and create a legally binding document that will stand up in court, if need be.

Ideally, it will be so robust that anyone reading the document will see the futility in contesting your wishes.

This is a good place to talk about contesting a Will or Trust. Any interested party can contest an Estate Plan if they think it was done illegally, meaning they think that you were under undue influence or duress or were not competent enough to prepare the plan. The concern should not be whether someone will contest your plan, but whether someone could win a contest of your plan. It should be immediately apparent why contesting a Trust Plan is far less likely to be successful. A Trust Plan is a living, breathing document from the moment you transfer your first asset into the name of the Trust. As you transfer additional assets, bank in the name of the trust, sign as Trustee of your trust, conduct business as Trustee of your trust, so on and so forth, for years and years, it is nearly impossible for someone to then say, "They didn't know what they were doing."

What Composes a Living Trust?

There are a number of documents that should be included in a good Trust Plan. They include the following:

- A good Table of Contents so you know where to find everything quickly

- A robust Trust Agreement with all the legal formalities to make it binding

- Successor Trustees confirmation documents

- Property Schedules listing assets transferred to the trust

- Personal Property Assignment agreement for the transfer of personal property to the trust

- Personal Property Memorandum for the disposition of certain personal property items

- A Trust Affidavit – privacy document confirming key details of your Trust for financial institutions

- A Trust Certification – supplemental privacy document certifying key details of your Trust for financial institutions

- A Trust Summary – short Article by Article description of Trust provisions

- Funding instructions for future asset transfers (the firm handling your estate plan should assist you with the initial asset transfer – this is VERY IMPORTANT)

- Trustee instructions for you and your Successor Trustee

Needless to say, a kit purchased online or at your local office supply store will not provide you with even a fraction of these items, nor will they be prepared in the detailed, case-specific manner in which you need them to be in order for them to serve their very important purpose. These documents are preserving hundreds of thousands of dollars worth of assets (maybe millions), so they need to be competently prepared by someone who knows what they are doing and is up-to-date with this ever-changing area of law.

When you lay your head down at night, you want to be able to breathe a sigh of relief, knowing that you have done all you can do to protect those you love. They will know it when they see the thought you put into their future care. It will put them on the path to do the same for their own family, so you will have left a legacy of care and financial wisdom for generations to come!

Chapter Six

Terms You Should Know

Here are a few terms and words that will definitely come up during your Estate Planning process, and also while constructing your Trust Plan. Get to know them and you will feel more comfortable with the entire process.

Advance Healthcare Directive

The document in which you name a person (your Agent) to make healthcare decisions on your behalf if you are incapacitated. You are called the Declarant in this document and it is only valid while you are alive.

Beneficiary

The person or persons named in a Trust or Will to receive assets or property, as decided by the owner of said property.

Bequeath/Bequest

The assets or property left to the beneficiary in a Will or Trust.

Codicil

The document used to edit or amend a Will.

Decedent

A person who has died.

Durable Power of Attorney

This document names the person (Agent or Attorney-in-Fact) who will handle financial matters for you (the Principal) if you are incapacitated. This document is only valid during the Principal's life.

Executor

The person who is designated to administer a Will or a decedent's estate by the court. The Executor is also known as the Personal Representative. This person will distribute the assets as laid out in the Will or intestacy law through the probate process.

Grantor/Settlor

The individual who creates a Trust. They can also amend a revocable Trust while they are alive and competent.

Intestate/intestacy

The term used when someone dies without a Will.

Irrevocable Trust

The type of Trust that cannot be changed once created. The Grantor loses control of the assets placed in an irrevocable trust.

Last Will and Testament

The legal document that outlines the beneficiaries of your assets, the Executor/Personal Representative of your probate estate, the guardian of your children, and your burial versus cremation and funeral wishes.

Legatee

The person bequeathed assets through a Will.

Letters of Administration

The legal document issued by the Register of Wills office through the Orphan's Court that gives your Executor or Personal Representative the power to act on behalf of your estate after your death.

Personal Representative

See Executor.

Restatement

The document used to revise or amend an existing Trust agreement. It keeps the name and date of the original Trust so that you do not have to retitle assets.

Revocable Living Trust

Also abbreviated as RLT, this type of Trust can be revised by the Grantor when they wish.

Standby Guardianship Designation

A guardian of minor children appointed for a short period of time (normally not longer than 6 months) until the official Guardian fills the role following the death or incapacitation of the parent/parents.

Testamentary Trust

A Trust that springs into existence after death, from the provisions contained in the person's Will.

Testator

A male person who creates a Will.

Testatrix

A female person who creates a Will.

Chapter Seven

The Simple Summary

In summary, this is a list of 10 key 'must-dos' and features when it comes to Estate Planning:

1. A GOOD Estate Plan creates the roadmap your loved ones can follow for things like: who you want to handle your medical and financial decisions if you can't; what you want that person to do and when; who should take care of your children if you can't and how they should be cared for; and how and when assets like life insurance should be distributed to your loved ones.

2. The primary goal of an Estate Plan is to make decisions about things concerning the management of your life, health and wealth while you are able to make those decisions. You then write out those decisions in a legally binding way so that what you **want** to happen actually **does** happen, rather than what the state legislature, court, or the loudest and bossiest family member decide should happen.

3. As with all the other areas of our lives, we need to put things in place to make sure that our loved ones and our things will be protected and, more importantly, that our plans, dreams and wishes are respected.

4. Without a good Estate Plan, your estate will have to go through probate. The primary reasons to avoid probate are: 1) it is time-consuming and delays distributions; 2) it is costly; and 3) it is public. However, probate can be completely avoided!

5. Create a GOOD Estate Plan by:

    a. Picking a reputable and experienced ESTATE-PLANNING attorney to prepare your Estate Plan.

    b. Be detailed about your family situation, assets and concerns when meeting with your attorney.

    c. Review and update your plan frequently.

6. A GOOD Estate Plan will include specific legally binding documents, such as a Durable Power of Attorney, an Advance Healthcare Directive and Living Will, a Last Will and Testament, and a Trust.

7. A Trust Plan is the best type of Estate Plan because it solves the problems of probate and intestacy laws – and has a ton of benefits too!

8. Estate planning is not just good stewardship of your finances; it is good stewardship of your relationships.

9. Estate-Planning documents preserve hundreds of thousands of dollars worth of assets (maybe millions), so they need to be competently prepared by someone who knows what they're doing and is up-to-date with this ever-changing area of law.

10. Leave a Legacy, not a Mess!

When you started on this journey of Estate Planning, you probably thought to yourself, "This is going to be complicated and cost me a fortune," but you can see that proper planning can actually save your estate thousands of dollars, while also protecting your assets and loved ones.

In my years as an attorney, I have met with many probate clients who have horrible family situations that could have been completely prevented by the establishment of a good estate plan. I have spoken with people who have lost family homes to foreclosure because they didn't know how to navigate the probate system. We all work hard to build a future for our loved ones, so why jeopardize what we have worked so hard to build by not working on a plan?

It is has been a privilege sharing this information with you. It is my earnest hope and prayer that everyone reading this will not only find value in the pages, but also be inspired to take action. Leaving a legacy for the next generation is not something for the few and the wealthy, but for all of us. So, I invite you to do just that – leave a legacy, not a mess!

www.ingramcontent.com/pod-product-compliance
Lightning Source LLC
Chambersburg PA
CBHW061224180526
45170CB00003B/1150